TRANSPARENCE OF THE WORLD

OTHER TRANSLATIONS BY W.S. MERWIN

*Asian Figures*

*East Window: The Asian Translations*

*Euripedes'* Iphigeneia at Aulis (with George E. Dimock, Jr.)

*Four French Plays*

*From the Spanish Morning*

*Lazarillo de Tormes*

*Osip Mandelstam: Selected Poems* (with Clarence Brown)

*Pieces of Shadow: Selected Poems of Jaime Sabines*

*The Poem of the Cid*

*Products of the Perfected Civilization: Selected Writings of Chamfort*

*Purgatorio* by Dante Alighieri

*The Satires of Persius*

*Selected Translations 1948–1968*

*Selected Translations 1968–1978*

*Sir Gawain and the Green Knight*

*The Song of Roland*

*Spanish Ballads*

*Sun at Midnight: Poems by Musō Soseki* (with Soiku Shigematsu)

*Twenty Love Poems and a Song of Despair* by Pablo Neruda

*Vertical Poetry: Poems by Roberto Juarroz*

*Voices* by Antonio Porchia

# TRANSPARENCE
# OF THE WORLD

### Jean Follain

*Selected and Translated*
*by W.S. Merwin*

Copper Canyon Press
Port Townsend, Washington

LIBRARY OF CONGRESS CATALOGING-IN-PUBLICATION DATA

Follain, Jean, 1903–1971
[Poems. English & French. Selections]
Transparence of the world / Jean Follain; selected and translated by
W.S. Merwin
     p.  cm.
Bilingual text in English and French.
ISBN 1-55659-190-X (alk. paper)
  1. Follain, Jean, 1903–1971—Translations into English.  I. Merwin,
W.S. (William Stanley), 1927–  II. Title.
PQ2611.0612A25 2003
841'.912—DC21

                                                          2002154701


COPPER CANYON PRESS
Post Office Box 271
Port Townsend, Washington 98368
www.coppercanyonpress.org

Copper Canyon Press is in residence under the auspices of the Centrum Foundation at Fort Worden State Park in Port Townsend, Washington. Centrum sponsors artist residencies, education workshops for Washington State students and teachers, Blues, Jazz, and Fiddle Tunes festivals, classical music performances, and the Port Townsend Writers' Conference.

# Contents

*xi*   *Preface*

*3*    Voluntary Mutilation

*5*    Landscape of a Child on His Way
       to the Place of the Regents

*7*    Appeal to the Red-Haired Soldiers

*9*    Death of a Ferret

*11*   Father and Daughter

*13*   Last Judgment

*15*   The Women Who Sew Livery

*17*   The Song of the Dragoon

*19*   Imperial Evenings

*21*   Free Growths

*23*   Preview of Death

*25*   Evenings of Ink

*27*   Dusk

*29*   Signs for Travellers

*31*   Speech Alone

*33*   The Beast

*35*   The Pyramid

*37*   Dawn

*39*   Housewives

*41*   The Barn-Owl

43  Existence

45  Matter

47  The Theater of *Tableaux Vivants*

49  The Useful

51  The Silence

53  Asia

55  The Secret

57  Domestic Life

59  The School and Nature

61  Death

63  The Egg

65  October Thoughts

67  The Students' Dog

69  The Plate

71  Humans

73  The Books and Love

75  Tragic Winter

77  Fraternities

79  Conspiracy

81  Life

83  The Woman and the Child in Costume

85  Wall

87  Trials

89  Cadences

91  The Voices

93   End of a Century

95   Another Time

97   Meal

99   The Evening Suit

101  Hollow Daydream

103  Show

105  The Square

107  Underground Palace

109  Couple

111  Signs

113  Eve

115  Exile

117  Black Meat

119  Imperial Hamlet

121  Solitaries

123  World's End

125  The Tragic in Time

127  Thief


129  *About the Author*

131  *About the Translator*

## Preface

In 1942 Jean Follain published a short volume of prose recalling in deliberate and composed detail the village of Canisy, in Normandy, where he had been born, and where many of his early childhood memories were rooted. The book is not a commentary on the poems, but it is (with his other prose writings) an agreeable and helpful relative, and they both set out from the same place. There are passages in *Canisy* that waken echoes in many of the poems:

> One evening during the 1914 war, while the stratus clouds built up in layers on the horizon, Mother Aimé, a washerwoman, standing on the doorsill talking to my maternal grandmother, was led to say, "This war will not be as bad as Napoleon's. It was bad at Berezina when the men and the horses died in piles. I had a great uncle who was there and told us."
>
> I looked intensely at the stones and the puddles on the road and I thought that the stones and puddles, on the eve of Berezina, must have been just as calm, just as interrogative and as ready to lose themselves in the shadow.
>
> When she had said, "Good-night, Madame," Mother Aimé left, one hand on her hip, and my grandmother began to close the white shutters that were held against the wall by fastenings in

the shape of busts of little people who looked
Italian in Renaissance feather bonnets.

The "I" is more openly present here than in the poems,
though even in *Canisy* it is never confronted but refers —
a regard. In this passage, and in much of Follain's prose, as
well as in his poems, the regard is suspended, whether de-
liberately or helplessly, and the complexity of its circum-
stances as the bearer or memory is clear. Who is the "I"
who is thinking those exact things about the puddles and
the shadows; and who recognizes that the shutter fasten-
ings in the shape of busts of little people were wearing
Renaissance feather bonnets? Is it the child of eleven or
so, or the man who left when that war was over, and has
gone to Paris and the legal profession, and the literary
world? It is more than both: it is the suspended regard
which they share, and the evocation of this "impersonal,"
receptive, but essentially unchanging gaze often occupies,
in Follain's work, the place of the first person.

It does so because memory has a special rôle in his
writing. It is not simply a link between past and present,
life and poetry. Memory, as distinct from the past it draws
on, is what makes the past a key to the mystery that stays
with us and does not change: the present. This office of
memory, quite apart from the attachment which Follain
has for particular objects of it, would have been grounds
for his statement that:

If you were commanded to forget certain things,
it would be better to be found like that man who

went mad as a result of his conscription under the Empire, among the moles and lizards around a dismantled belfry.

This is doubly so because Follain's concern is finally with the mystery of the present—the mystery which gives the recalled concrete details their form, at once luminous and removed, when they are seen at last in their places, as they seem to be in the best of his poems. This is their value "in themselves." At the same time it is what gives them the authority of parts of a rite, of an unchanging ceremony heralding some inexorable splendor, over a ground of silence. And for Follain it is a fulfillment not only of a need for ceremony but of a fondness for the ceremonious, in which each detail, seen as itself, is an evocation of the processions of an immeasurable continuum.

And both the passage of time and the sense of the unchanging show the details to be unique. Follain never regarded them otherwise—that is the child whom he did not betray. He spoke with a shudder of the possibility of having been born even a year or so later (his birth date was August 29, 1903) and so not being able to remember the whole existence that, as he testifies, vanished with the 1914–1918 war. And when, in 1919, he was sent to England (Leeds) to learn the language, his resistance to the enterprise took the form of a refusal to believe that there was more than one way of naming a thing. The language, the words, in which he had learned to name particulars, were part of the uniqueness of the things named. Every morning he read a French newspaper—dull, but the only one available that did not speak in a language that was mere analogy.

In Paris, in the mid-twenties, his life and his literary beginnings were both quiet. He associated first with a group that included Erik Satie, Max Jacob, Pierre Reverdy, and Léon-Paul Fargue, and in 1933 he brought out his first substantial collection of poems, *La Main chaude* (five had been published earlier, in a small edition, and others had appeared in literary reviews). After that date he published a succession of books of poems and (after 1935, when *Paris* appeared) of prose pieces whose aim, as in *Canisy*, is to conjure the sense of specific recollections of places, occasions, objects. In some collections poems and prose were published together.

For many years he served as magistrate in a small town in Normandy, travelling back and forth from Paris, where he lived in an ancient, rambling apartment in the Place des Vosges. When he retired, the town had his judicial summaries printed and elaborately bound "since"—as they explained when they presented the volume to him—"he was a man of letters." He loved to demonstrate the ritual with which a provincial magistrate closed the judicial year and then opened the new one at the same session. He also loved to eat, devoted an affectionate small book to the potato, maintained a careful list of favorite restaurants in Paris, and was on his way to one of them to dine with friends, when he was killed by a car on the Place de la Concorde.

—*W.S. Merwin*

TRANSPARENCE OF THE WORLD

## Mutilation volontaire

Pour s'éviter de servir
aux armées de l'empereur,
un beau soir avec la hache
le maître se mutila
de deux grands doigts de sa main,
sa jeune et blonde épouse
pansa la plaie tendrement
et les pensées à coeur jaune
tremblèrent dans le parterre
les deux chiens du maître hurlèrent
quand on le porta au lit
alors charbonnaient les lampes
entourées de papillons;
mais les femmes assemblées
sur la place du village
devant la rougeur des nuages
disaient que ce qu'elles voyaient
était le sang des soldats.

## Voluntary Mutilation

Rather than have to serve
in the emperor's armies
one fine evening the master
took the ax to himself
cut from his hand two great fingers,
his young blonde wife
gently bandaged the place
and the yellow hearted
pansies shook in the border
the master's two dogs howled
as he was carried to bed
then the lamps smoked
surrounded by moths
but the women who gathered
on the village square
facing the red clouds said
that what they saw was the blood
of soldiers.

*Paysage de l'enfant allant chez les régents*

Ce grand silence liquide
habitant les tonneaux
ces minuscules insectes
s'essayant en vain à dévorer la peau des vierges
les charrons buvant près du chardon bleu
les frelons fabriquant leur miel blanc
l'abeille distillant son miel blond
les chaudrons fulgurants
que l'on frotte de cendre mouillée
les bruits de fin d'orage
l'âcre fumée
de la mauvaise herbe brûlée
en tas dans les jardins à buis
et le portrait d'un roi
au mur de la cuisine
et l'argile et le plâtre
dans les royaumes humides,
Tout est Courrier d'une impossible aurore;
voilà qu'elle est déjà tout en haut de la côte
la veuve
qui conduit par la main jusqu'au lointain collège
l'enfant à tignasse rouge.

*Landscape of a Child on His Way*
*to the Place of the Regents*


This great liquid silence
inhabiting the barrels
these tiny insects
trying in vain to devour the skin of virgins
the wheelwrights drinking near the blue thistle
the hornets making their white honey
the bees distilling their blond honey
the flashing cauldrons
that are rubbed with wet ashes
the sounds of the storm's end
the rank smoke
of weeds burning in piles
in box-hedged gardens
and the portrait of a king
on the kitchen wall
and the clay and plaster
in the damp kingdoms:
All of it is the Messenger of an impossible dawn:
there she is already at the top of the hill
the widow
leading by the hand to the distant school
the child with the wild red hair.

*Appel aux soldats roux*

Le chef franc porté sur un pavois
par des soldats roux
a laissé dans la terre,
souvenir chrétien,
un morceau du pot où il buvait;
l'on nous dit ses fils
de par l'arbre identique
de par le même oiseau
mais à l'heure où l'on se mire
quand le bois de nos meubles travaille
dans un appartement sans rats,
sans champignons
aux joints du parquet neuf
et qu'il n'y a même pas
un gant embaumé
l'on se sent seul alors
ô soldats roux.

## Appeal to the Red-Haired Soldiers

The chief of the Franks borne on a shield
by red-haired soldiers
has left in the earth
a Christian souvenir
a piece of the jug he drank from;
it is said that we are his sons
from the identical tree
from the same bird
but at the hour when we look at ourselves
and the wood of the furniture gives
in an apartment without rats
without rot
with new joints in the flooring
and without even
a scented glove
then one feels alone
O red-haired soldiers.

## Mort du furet

Entré dans un terrier, il pénétra jusqu'au lapin hagard
suça son sang
s'en saoula, s'endormit;
la fumée des feux de brandes
allumés par les paysans chiches
qui parlent par monosyllabes
ne le réveilla pas
d'une mortelle torpeur.
Sur le chemin s'en revenaient ces petites filles
aux coeurs à nervures aussi nettes
que celles des feuilles du lilas.
Le lapin saigné demeura sans odeur
mais les furets dès qu'irrités
dégagent une morne puanteur
qui survit tristement après leur mort crépusculaire.

## Death of a Ferret

Inside a burrow, he
made his way to the haggard rabbit
sucked its blood
gorged, bloated, fell asleep;
the smoke of heather fires
lit by close-fisted peasants
who talked in monosyllables
failed to rouse him
from a fatal lethargy.
On the road those little girls
with hearts as clearly veined
as lilac leaves
were coming back.
The bled rabbit remained odorless
but ferrets when vexed
give off a gloomy stench
which lingers on sadly after their twilit death.

*Père et fille*

Elle naquit entourée des redingotes noires
des docteurs qui pratiquèrent la césarienne,
sa mère mourut,
son père garda sa voix tonnante,
il agrippait de ses longs doigts
le bord des tables fileté d'or
quand il discutait avec les cardinaux;
seul quelquefois il gémissait
couvert de lueurs par le soleil couchant
et la manchette hors de la manche
égarait ses regards sur les vases de Chine
mais sa fille
ne fit jamais que peu de bruit
près des longues fenêtres, elle cousait
nimbée à la couleur du jour
ses doigts aux ongles sans envie
fronçaient de légères étoffes
qu'elle déchirait entre ses dents.

## Father and Daughter

She was born in the midst of the black frock-coats
of the doctors who performed the caesarean,
her mother died,
her father kept his thunderous voice,
he gripped in his long fingers
the edges of tables ruled in gold
during his discussions with the cardinals;
alone at times he groaned
covered with patches of light by the setting sun
and with his cuff out of his sleeve
his glances would wander over the Chinese vases
but his daughter
at no time made much noise
by the long windows she sewed
haloed in the color of the day
her fingers with their desireless nails
gathered light fabrics
which she tore with her teeth.

## Jugement Dernier

à André Mora

Le chantre impotent tout l'été
près des fumiers et des roses
et Léopold qui dormait dans l'étable
à cause de ses chancres
et tous les autres
les voilà en la vallée de Josaphat
et le chapier voit sans comprendre
les plantes dont parlaient ses psaumes;
tous les villages sont au ciel
groupés autour du clocher.

## Last Judgment

for André Mora


The chorister crippled all summer
beside the manure piles and roses
and Leopold who slept in the stable
because of his canker-sores
and all the others
there they are in the valley of Jehoshaphat
and the wearer of vestments sees without understanding
the plants spoken of in the psalms;
all the villages are in heaven
gathered around the steeple.

## Les Couseuses de livrées

Les couseuses de livrées
s'arrêtent à la nuit venue
attendant qu'on leur donne la lumière voulue.
La ville est couverte de neige,
alors elles chantent
et le passant entend dans la rue sans oiseaux
monter chaudes et bien timbrées
les voix de ces filles à vêtir les valets
et s'en va triste et seul
à des tablées fantômes.

## The Women Who Sew Livery

When night falls
the women who sew livery
stop and wait to be given the light they wish for.
The town is covered with snow,
it is then that they sing
and the passer-by hears in the birdless street
the warm clear voices rising
from those girls who make clothes for valets
and he goes off sad and alone
to phantom dinners.

## Le Chant du dragon

Guêtres de cuir noir aux jambes fines
de ce garçon,
ragoût amer
que laissèrent brûler, ô femme vos mains blanches
et qu'il mange
avec une fourchette d'étain
au milieu des lueurs éternelles
et l'on voit remuer ses longs cils
l'on voit ses boutons blancs
lutter contre la nuit
puis l'on entend sa toux songeuse
qui se mêle aux abois
de grands chiens aux poils violacés
leurs gueules vers les étoiles.
C'est alors que dragon du convoi
il se lève et va vers les autres
assis sur les puits
et seul il entonne la romance qui monte
et fait sous le large ciel vert
trembler les rats dans leur royaume.

## The Song of the Dragoon

Black leather leggings
on that boy's slender legs,
bitter stew
which your white hands, O woman, let burn,
and which he eats
with a pewter fork
in the midst of the eternal lights
and his long lashes can be seen moving
and his white buttons
contending against the night
and his pensive cough can be heard
mingled with the barking
of the great purple-furred dogs
muzzles turned toward the stars.
It is then that he the convoy's dragoon
rises and approaches the others
sitting on the wells
and all by himself intones the ballad that rises
and under the green heaven makes
the rats tremble in their kingdom.

*Soirs impériaux*


Les empereurs n'ont pas toujours revêtu
des atours frais,
mais parfois de grands cordons fanés
et des chapeaux d'usure luisants
sur le seuil des fermes
aux fins rouges des jours.
Pendant ce temps mélancoliques des enfants
s'amusaient avec des vers de terre
devant l'eau morte aux mousses d'or,
les abeilles ne bourdonnaient plus,
l'ivrogne parlait au taillis
qui s'engloutissait dans la nuit
en rassemblant ses noires vertèbres.

## Imperial Evenings

The emperors have not always donned fresh attire,
but sometimes faded ribbons
and hats worn till they shone
on the door-sills of farms
in the red ends of days.
During those melancholy times the children
amused themselves with earthworms
in front of the stagnant water frothed with gold,
the bees hummed no longer,
the drunkard talked to the thicket
that was being swallowed up by the night
as he reassembled his black vertebrae.

## Libres croissances

Il est au fond du sang des végétations folles
qui de jour et de nuit
poussent de fines épines
jusque chez les soldats
aux haves bourgerons.
Alors hennissent au loin les juments de légende
et les doux enfants rentrent avec des pains immenses
crevassés de grands yeux
et couturés de croix
et tout blessés d'étoiles.
Alors semblent d'accord s'élever vers le ciel
des jardins en broussailles
avec des statues blanches
des prés pharamineux
abandonnés des hommes,
et des laitières pâmées au pied des églantiers
les lèvres en feu
l'azur aux yeux.

## Free Growths

At the bottom of the blood there is rank vegetation
from which day and night
fine thorns grow
all the way to the soldiers
in the wan buds.
Then the mares of legend whinny in the distance
and the gentle children come back with immense loaves
split with huge eyes
scarred with crosses
all wounded with stars.
Then the brush-grown gardens seem
to rise as with one accord toward heaven
with white statues
and prodigious meadows
abandoned by men,
and milkmaids swooning at the feet of eglantines
their lips on fire
the azure in their eyes.

## Aperception de la mort

Quand les maisons se penchent un peu
des filles aux fenêtres se montrent
tandis qu'au fond d'une pièce noire
luit le peu d'or d'une montre
suspendue au clou rouillé
et les vengeances au faubourg
font jaser;
la marâtre arrive
et sourit tenant des lilas,
chacun a fortement prédit
que bientôt enfin elle sera
prête pour la fosse commune.
Savates à la crasse cirée
vous serez sur le carreau rouge
dépossédées de ses pieds noirs,
prises de l'hirsute chiffonnier
ou jeu de quelque chat sauvage,
savates vous irez rejoindre
un amas de vieux étendards
tandis qu'elle ne sera plus là
cachant des lettres en son corsage
épiant les démolitions
dans le quartier qu'on reconstruit
et criant un pain sous son bras
à l'entour des mortiers fumants.

## Preview of Death

When the houses lean slightly
girls can be seen in the windows
while far back in a black room
the small gold of a watch gleams
hanging on a rusty nail
and the neighborhood revenges
set tongues wagging;
the stepmother arrives
and smiles holding pieces of lilac,
everyone has said
that it won't be long now
before she's ready at last
for the common grave.
Old shoes with the dirt polished
you will be on the red square
dispossessed of your black feet,
seized by the hairy ragman
or toys of some homeless cat,
old shoes you will go to join
a heap of old flags
when she is no longer there
hiding letters in her blouse
spying on the demolitions
in the area being rebuilt
and wailing
with a loaf of bread under her arm
around the smoking piles of mortar.

## Soirs d'encre

Obsédant souvenir des contacts
premiers,
c'était le frémissement des tiges
et des feuilles dans le jardin
aux sournois jours de cendre.
Taches d'encre
dans les soirs rouges
alors que tremblaient les bêtes;
taches qui s'étoilaient
sur le maigre papier des cahiers froids.
Immenses brumes autour des femmes,
elles allaient
saluant les croix rongées.
Encre dont il revoit les sels verts,
quand ses yeux se fatiguent,
quand sa gorge est amère.
Encre d'apparat
dans le bourg envieux.

## Evenings of Ink

Obsessive memory of first
contacts,
it was the rustling of twigs
and leaves in the garden
in the sullen days of ash.
Spots of ink
in the red evenings
while the beasts trembled;
spots that ran into stars
on the thin paper of cold notebooks.
Immense fogs around women,
they went
greeting the gnawed crosses.
Ink whose green salts he sees again
when his eyes grow tired,
when his throat is bitter.
Sumptuous ink
in the envious town.

*Entre chien et loup*


C'est l'heure où le fils rentre
et voit d'abord sur la crédence
le pardessus, le chapeau haut
comme autant de royaux insignes
et dehors le parterre est noir,
il y a deux grands souliers béants
qu'ont ravagés les jours pluvieux
et qui ont été
jetés l'un après l'autre
du geste égaré d'un soucieux
d'un père athée
qui ne voit que vide au fond des cieux.

## Dusk

The hour "between dog and wolf"

It is the hour when the son comes in
and sees at once on the side-table
the top-coat, the tall hat
like so many royal emblems
and outside the flower-bed is black,
there are two great shoes gaping
that were ravaged by days of rain
and have been tossed there
one after the other
by the vague gesture of an anxious
an atheist father
who sees only a void in the depths of the heavens.

## Signes pour voyageurs

Voyageurs des grands espaces
lorsque vous verrez une fille
tordant dans des mains de splendeur
une chevelure immense et noire
et que par surcroît
vous verrez
près d'une boulangerie sombre
un cheval couché dans la mort
à ces signes vous reconnaîtrez
que vous êtes parmi les hommes.

## Signs for Travellers

Travellers from the great spaces
when you see a girl
twisting in sumptuous hands
the black vastness of her hair
and when moreover
you see
near a dark baker's
a horse lying near death
by these signs you will know
that you have come among men.

*Parler seul*


Il arrive que pour soi
l'on prononce quelques mots
seul sur cette étrange terre
alors la fleurette blanche
le caillou semblable à tous ceux du passé
la brindille de chaume
se trouvent réunis
au pied de la barrière
que l'on ouvre avec lenteur
pour rentrer dans la maison d'argile
tandis que chaises, table, armoire
s'embrasent d'un soleil de gloire.

## Speech Alone

It happens that one pronounces
a few words just for oneself
alone on this strange earth
then the small white flower
the pebble like all those that went before
the sprig of stubble
find themselves re-united
at the foot of the gate
which one opens slowly
to enter the house of clay
while chairs, table, cupboard
blaze in a sun of glory.

*La Bête*


Assise en un corps de logis
où conduisent d'anciens chemins
vit une bête
qui n'attend rien du monde
des pièces communiquent
des portes se ferment
et des nuits s'approchent
dans le parfum d'un acacia.
Toutes les bêtes de son espèce
vivent en elle.

## The Beast

Sitting in an apartment house
where ancient paths lead
a beast lives
who expects nothing from the world
the rooms connect
the doors close
and nights come near
in the smell of an acacia.
All the beasts of her species
live in her.

## La Pyramide

Rue Saint-Honoré, en hommage
les indigents élevèrent au roi Louis-Seize
une pyramide de neige
et pour la voir il traversa la foule
où se cachaient des frappes et des goules
la nuit allait tomber
le soir tissait ses givres
une sombre beauté
apparaissait chez quelques filles soumises.
Le roi Louis marchant à l'échafaud
dans son habit blanc
gardait le souvenir des ombres d'un hiver.

## The Pyramid


Rue Saint-Honoré, in homage
the paupers raised to King Louis the Sixteenth
a pyramid of snow
and to see it he made his way through the crowd
where cut-throats and vampires were hiding
night was about to fall
the evening was weaving its frosts
on a few humble girls
a somber beauty appeared.
King Louis walking to the scaffold
in his white coat
remembered a winter's shadows.

## L'Aube

Un toit de maison puis l'étoile
au-dessus pâlissante
arrêtaient les regards d'un homme
qui se sentait repris par le fin jeu des causes
plus bas les enseignes
dévoilaient leurs mots d'or
le bois, le fer, la pierre
imposaient leur présence
une fenêtre grande ouverte
montrait le mur d'ocre et l'armoire
et la main qui posait une cuiller de fer
sur la faïence d'une assiette
â l'ancien ébrèchement.

## Dawn

A house roof and the star
growing pale above it
held the glance of a man
who felt himself caught again
in the delicate play of causes
the signs farther down
disclosed their golden words
the wood, the iron, the stone
enforced their presence
a wide open window
showed the ochre wall and the cupboard
and the hand laying an iron spoon
on the china of a plate
where it was chipped long ago.

## Les Ménagères

Des ménagères aux nuits montantes
disaient n'avoir rien fait du jour
et sur son lit un moribond
les entendait;
l'une parlait d'une voix cristalline
et son corps d'une beauté grave
portait dans ses bras un enfant
à bavoir à rubans ternis
et qui toussait aux fumées
montant des feux brûlant l'herbe
dans un jardin silencieux.
Jusqu'aux derniers chants des oiseaux
s'étant longuement plaintes
elles se quittaient enfin
pour jeter le sel
à leur bouillon du soir.

## Housewives

Housewives as the nights came in
said they'd done nothing with the day
and on his bed the man dying
heard them;
one spoke in a crystalline voice
and her body with its grave beauty
carried in its arms a child
in a bib with faded ribbons
coughing at the gusts of smoke
from the weeds burning
in a silent garden.
Having long aired their complaints
until the last bird song
they separated at last
to salt
their evening broth.

## L'Effraie

On dit que l'effraie
boit l'huile aux lampes du sanctuaire
dans les églises de village;
elle entre par le vitrail brisé
dans ces heures de nuit
quand les bons et les violents s'endorment
quand l'orgueil et l'amour s'épuisent
quand le feuillage rêve.
La bête réchauffe son sang
avec l'huile éclairante et vierge.

## The Barn-Owl

They say that the barn-owl
drinks the oil of the sanctuary lamps
in the village churches;
she comes in through a broken pane
during the night hours
when the good and the violent are sleeping
when pride and love are worn out
when the foliage dreams.
The beast warms her blood
with the virgin light-giving oil.

## L'Existence

L'homme aux politiques sombres
dans un boudoir bouton d'or
vit se dénouer un chignon noir
les cheveux roulèrent comme un gave
dans ce gave croulaient des roses
et dans une rose l'insecte muet
n'abdiquait pas son existence
et gravissait seul doucement
le pétale ému de la fleur
cueillie aux ravins de la mort
au cours d'une longue journée.

*Existence*


The man of dark politics
in a gold-buttoned boudoir
watched the untying of a black chignon
the hair rolled out like a torrent
in the torrent roses tumbled
and in one rose the mute insect
would not abdicate its existence
and clambered alone slowly
on the trembling petal of the flower
plucked from the ravines of death
in the course of a long day.

## La Matière

Sur la matière
plane un rêve
mais esclave
chez un maître infâme
le vase de verre
porte une rose sombre
l'or rutile
et le fer rouge
fait hurler la beauté
fragile et nue
dans la nuit de l'être.
Réduites aux choses
de fourrures mortes
pendent au mur blême.

## Matter

Above matter
a dream floats
a slave
in the house of an infamous master
the glass vase
holds a dark rose
the gold turns rusty
and the red iron
makes the frail naked beauty
howl
in the night of being.
Reduced to things
dead furs
hang on the pallid wall.

## Le Théâtre des tableaux vivants

Un homme s'arrêta voir les tableaux vivants
dans un théâtre aujourd'hui mort
ô mains, ô coeurs, ô veines fines
des femmes exposées en silence!
les dorures du plafond
les cariatides énormes
encadraient leurs chairs de mères;
le décor était un faux printemps;
pas un seul cri d'enfant
ne remuait l'assemblée
et dehors tous les toits s'étaient couverts de neige.

# *The Theater of* Tableaux Vivants

A man stopped to see the *tableaux vivants*
in a theater that today is dead
O hands, O hearts, O fine veins
of women exposed in silence!
the gildings of the ceiling
the enormous caryatids
framed their maternal flesh;
the backdrop showed a false springtime;
not one child's cry
troubled the gathering
and outside all the roofs were covered with snow.

## L'Utile

Dans les couleurs de l'utile
celle de l'étoffe grise et noire
de l'acier bleu
des graines rousses
d'aucuns se réfugient pour vivre.

On entend parfois leurs paroles
les appels qu'ils font à la pluie
au soleil, aux verdures

et les choses autour d'eux se joignent
pour se refléter dans leurs yeux.

## The Useful

In the colors of the useful
that of gray and black material
of steel blue
of rusty flecks
some take shelter in order to live.

Sometimes one hears their words
their appeals to the rain
to the sun, to green leaves

and the things around them unite
to be reflected in their eyes.

## Le Silence

Au fond du temps verdoie un merveilleux silence
fait avec les bourgs, les villes, et les coteaux
il dort et s'accomplit
il épuise une pierre
et celle-ci tombe un soir d'hiver
sur une femme étrangère
aux seins couleur d'opale
qu'enferme du drap rouge.
Avec la femme meurent d'infimes bêtes
une fleur, un oiseau, un calvaire
écrasés par la même pierre.

## The Silence

In the depths of time a marvellous silence turns green
made of the cities, the towns, and the slopes
it sleeps and is accomplished
it exhausts a stone
which falls one winter evening
on a foreign woman
with breasts the color of opal
enclosed in red fabric.
With the woman die tiny beasts
a flower, a bird, a crucifix,
crushed by the same stone.

*L'Asie*

Par la fenêtre de l'école
on voyait la carte d'Asie
la Sibérie y était aussi chaude que l'Inde
les insectes y cheminaient
de l'Indus au fleuve Amour;
au pied du mur
un homme mangeait sa soupe
que les fèves rendaient mauve
il était grave
et seul au monde.

## Asia

Through the window of the school
the map of Asia could be seen
Siberia was as warm as India
the insects made their way
from the Indus to the Amour River;
at the foot of the wall
a man was eating his soup
which the beans had turned mauve
he was grave
and alone in the world.

## Le Secret

Où gis-tu secret du monde
à l'odeur si puissante?
Parfois un ouvrier doux
dans la ville fiévreuse
tombe d'un échafaudage
et le vent sent toujours le lilas;
un malheur tenace
habite les corps les plus beaux
les mains dans le soir se serrent
un animal s'endort
dans une loge qu'ouvragèrent les hommes
la paix toujours se corrompt
et la guerre
n'a plus d'âge.

## The Secret

Where are you lying
secret of the world
with so strong an odor?
Sometimes a gentle workman
in the feverish town
falls from a scaffolding
and the wind goes on smelling of lilac;
a tenacious misfortune
lodges in the loveliest bodies
hands tighten in the evening
an animal sleeps
within walls worked over by men
peace decays forever
and war no longer
has an age.

## La Vie domestique

La femme se lavait et regardait l'attelage
nul bocage n'eût gardé sa peau fraîche
la mort survenue
et la vie domestique entière apparaissait
liée au passé du monde
végétaux qu'on gratte ou pèle
pour en nourrir les filles belles
pierre longuement balayée
dans l'été blond
animaux saignés au grand jour
et dont le cri strident
se perd dans la lumière.

## Domestic Life

The woman washing herself watched the team in harness
no thicket would have protected her skin's freshness
sudden death
and the whole of domestic life
seemed bound up in the world's past
vegetables that are scraped or peeled
to nourish beautiful girls
stone swept a long time
in the blond summer
animals bled in broad day
whose grating cry
is lost in the light.

*L'Ecole et la nature*

Intact sur le tableau
dans la classe d'un bourg
un cercle restait tracé
et la chaire était désertée
et les élèves étaient partis
l'un d'eux naviguant sur le flot
un autre labourant seul
et la route allait serpentant
un oiseau y faisant tomber
les gouttes sombres de son sang.

## The School and Nature

Drawn on the blackboard
in the classroom in a town
a circle remained intact
and the teacher's chair was deserted
and the students had gone
one sailing on the flood
another plowing alone
and the road went winding
a bird letting fall
the dark drops of its blood.

*La mort*

Avec les os de bêtes,
l'usine avait fabriqué ces boutons
qui fermaient
un corsage sur un buste
d'ouvrière éclatante
lorsqu'elle tomba
l'un des boutons se défit dans la nuit
et le ruisseau des rues
alla le déposer
jusque dans un jardin privé
où s'effritait
une statue en plâtre de Pomone
rieuse et nue.

*Death*


From the bones of animals
the factory had made these buttons
which fastened
a bodice over the bust
of a gorgeous working-girl
when she fell
one of the buttons came off in the night
and the water of the gutters took it
and laid it down
in a private garden
with a crumbling plaster statue
Pomona
naked and laughing.

## L'Oeuf

La vieille dame essuie un oeuf
avec son tablier d'usage
oeuf couleur ivoire et lourd
que nul ne lui revendique
puis elle regarde l'automne
par la petite lucarne
et c'est comme un tableau fin
aux dimensions d'une image
rien n'y est
hors de saison
et l'oeuf fragile
que dans sa paume elle tient
reste la seul objet neuf.

## The Egg

The old woman dried an egg
with her working apron
heavy egg the color of ivory
which nobody claims from her
then she looks at the autumn
through the little dormer
and it is like a fine painting
the size of a picture book
nothing is
out of season
and the fragile egg
that she holds in her palm
remains the one thing that is new.

*Pensées d'octobre*

On aime bien
ce grand vin
que l'on boit solitaire
quand le soir illumine les collines cuivrées
plus un chasseur n'ajuste
les gibiers de la plaine
les soeurs de nos amis
apparaissent plus belles
il y a pourtant menace de guerre
un insecte s'arrête
puis repart.

## October Thoughts

How one loves
this great wine
that one drinks all alone
when the evening illumines its coppered hills
not a hunter now
stalks the lowland game
the sisters of our friends
seem more beautiful
at the same time there is a threat of war
an insect pauses
then goes on.

## Chien aux écoliers

Les écoliers par jeu brisent la glace
dans un sentier
près du chemin de fer
on les a lourdement habillés
d'anciens lainages sombres
et ceinturés de cuirs fourbus
le chien qui les suit
n'a plus d'écuelle où manger tard
il est vieux
car il a leur âge.

## The Students' Dog

The students play at breaking the ice
on a path
near the railroad
they have been wrapped up warm
in old dark woolens
and belted in with bossed leather
the dog that follows them
no longer has a bowl for his late meals
he is old
their age.

## L'Assiette

Quand tombe des mains de la servante
la pâle assiette ronde
de la couleur des nuées
il en faut ramasser les débris,
tandis que frémit le lustre
dans la salle à manger des maîtres
et que la vieille école ânonne
une mythologie incertaine
dont on entend
quand le vent cesse
nommer tous les faux dieux.

## The Plate

When the serving girl's hands
drop the pale round plate
the color of clouds
the pieces have to be picked up
while the light trembles overhead
in the masters' dining room
and the old school stammers
an uncertain mythology
in which one hears the names
when the wind stops
of all the false gods.

*Humains*


Des hommes bruns ou blonds
noirs ou rouges
ont pris par un chemin glacé
on veut les revoir ils sont morts.
Par ces temps douteux de pays tempérés
ils firent voir
dans une éclaircie
un bijou d'argent ou d'or
alors qu'ils regardaient les prés
ou quelque village d'abeilles
rappelant les huttes gauloises
à l'écolier fiévreux
qu'ils tenaient ferme par la main.

*Humans*


Men with brown hair blond hair
black hair red hair
have taken an icy path
it would be good to see them again they are dead.
In this shifting weather of temperate countries
they revealed
when the sky cleared once
a jewel of silver or gold
while they watched the pastures
or some village of bees that looked
like the huts of the Gauls
to the feverish student
whom they held firmly by the hand.

*Les Livres et l'amour*

Les livres dont s'emplit la chambre
comme des harpes éoliennes s'émeuvent
quand passe le vent venu des orangers
et la lettre dans la page incrustée
se retient
au blanc papier de lin
et la guerre au loin tonne
dans cet automne flamboyant
tuant la maîtresse avec l'amant
au bord d'un vieux rivage.

## The Books and Love

The books that fill the room
are moved like aeolian harps
when the wind passes on its way from the orange trees
and the letter incrusted in the page
clings
to the white linen paper
and the war thunders in the distance
in this blazing autumn
killing the mistress and the lover
on an old shore.

## Tragique hiver

Plus de berger à l'horizon
s'appuyant sur le roc à fleurs minuscules
on balayait les maisons
des familles silencieuses
dont les filles à corsage étroit
au visage strictement nu
avec des bâillements montraient
le rose de leur palais
peu soucieuses d'une beauté
attachée aux mêmes rivages.

## Tragic Winter

Not one shepherd
left on the horizon
leaning on the rock with its tiny flowers
from the houses
the silent families have been swept
with their narrow-bosomed daughters
whose faces severely naked
displayed in yawning
the pink roofs of their mouths
and their small heed of a beauty
tied to those same shores.

*Fraternités*

Quand le voleur de voitures
rencontre le voleur de chevaux
ils mangent lentement,
la sauce dans leurs assiettes à fêlures
doucement se fige
ils voient dans la brume
la statue équestre de la place
près des étriers de granit
plus grands que nature
des couples échangent
leurs mots clairs.

*Fraternities*

When the carriage thief
meets the horse thief
they eat slowly,
the sauce on their cracked plates
gradually congeals
they see in the mist
the equestrian statue in the square
by the granite stirrups
larger than life
couples exchange
their clear words.

## Conspiration

Les glaces reflètent
des glaives et trophées
chrétienne elle se défait
de sa robe écumeuse
pleine d'agrafes, de rubans, de noeuds
puis de tout son corps tendu
écoute la vie en elle
mais les âmes
de la conspiration
veillent à travers les piliers
et le cri survenu du porteur d'eau
fait éclater l'or d'un silence païen.

## Conspiracy

The mirrors reflect
swords and trophies
she a Christian
divests herself
of her frothy gown
all clasps ribbons knots
then listens with her whole body tensed
to the life in her
but the souls
of the conspiracy
are watching from behind pillars
and the water carrier's sudden cry
shatters the gold of a pagan silence.

*Vie*

Il naît un enfant
dans un grand paysage
un demi-siècle après
il n'est qu'un soldat mort
et c'était là cet homme
que l'on vit apparaître
et puis poser par terre
tout un lourd sac de pommes
dont deux ou trois roulèrent
bruit parmi ceux d'un monde
où l'oiseau chantait
sur la pierre du seuil.

*Life*


A child is born
in a vast landscape
half a century later
he is simply a dead soldier
and that was the man
whom one saw appear
and set down on the ground a whole
heavy sack of apples
two or three of which rolled
a sound among the sounds of a world
where the bird sang
on the stone of the door-sill.

## La Femme et l'enfant travestie

Courageuse aux coups du destin
un soir de carnaval une femme
par la main tenait une enfant
travestie en folie
les grands monuments s'étendaient
devant leur marche vive
et les grelots sonnaient
sur l'habit mi-partie
rouge et jaune
de la fillette pâle autant que le ciel.

## The Woman and the Child in Costume

Brave under the blows of fate
one evening a woman
led a child by the hand
to the carnival
dressed as Folly
the great monuments stretched ahead
before their brisk pace
and the small bells tinkled
on the costume half red
half yellow
of the little girl as pale as the sky.

## Muraille

C'est un moellon violâtre
mal pris dans son ciment
qui se fend sous le gel
mais se tiendra l'ensemble
alors l'homme simple
qui à chaque aurore
tourne la clef dans la serrure
contourne son parterre
jette un os au chien noir
mourra seul collé contre son mur
en voyant des fumées
aux horizons fuyants.

## Wall

It is a purplish stone
loose in its cement
that cracks in the frost
but the rest will hold up
so the simple man
who at every sunrise
turns the key in the lock
walks around his flower-bed
throws a bone to the black dog
will die alone stuck against his wall
seeing columns of smoke
on the fleeing horizons.

*Epreuves*

Aux confins du jardin la campagne commence
sur le large établi
tremblent les lueurs de la tenaille
le malheur s'installe
au pied d'un arbre
les animaux tournent leur tête vers qui va pleurer
des mains se joignent
dans un désespoir légendaire
de la cuisine vient l'odeur des ferments
dans la boîte restée ouverte
le cirage est devenu un dur disque noir;
sèche au soleil
la glaise des greffes.

*Trials*

Beyond the garden the country begins
on the wide work bench
the bright pincers glitter
misfortune settles itself
at the foot of a tree
the animals turn their heads
toward the one who is about to cry
hands clasp in a despair out of legends
from the kitchen comes the smell of fermenting
in the can left open
the wax has become a hard black disk;
in the sun the clay
dries on the grafts.

## Cadences

La mer reste aussi grise
que la pierre tombale
le régiment des folles
rentre dans sa demeure
avec des mots sans suite
mais la lettre s'inscrit
sur le livre oublié.
On entend des fléaux
qui battent du blé maigre
en de sourdes cadences
par un soir que la pluie
ne menace le terre
doucement réchauffée.

# *Cadences*

The sea remains
as gray as the tombstone
the regiment of madwomen
re-enters its building
with words that have no thread
but the letter is inscribed
on the forgotten book.
A sound of flails
threshing thin wheat
in muffled cadences
comes in the evening
over the warmed earth
unthreatened by rain.

## Les Voix

Sur les boulevards des villes
près des croix de faubourg
à l'intérieur des murs desséchés
on entend appeler
le nom qui se prolonge
quelqu'un parfois répond
pris au charme de la parole
assoiffé de vérité peut-être;
il arrive aussi qu'une bataille de chiens
sur le parvis d'une vieille église
empêche d'entendre de lointains cris
qui alors se perdent dans la mort

## The Voices

On the boulevards of towns
near the neighborhood crosses
within powdery walls
can be heard the calling
of a name long drawn out
sometimes someone answers
caught by the charm of the word
or perhaps thirsting for truth;
but other times a dog fight
in the square in front of an old church
keeps one from hearing cries in the distance
which are then lost in death.

*Fin de siècle*


Une mouche marchait sur l'initiale
d'un drap lourd de silence
on éveilla l'enfant
un trente et un décembre
pour qu'il pût voir la fin d'un siècle
des visages épuisés
s'en adoucirent aux lueurs des flammes;
fronces, guipures, tresses
résisteraient des mois encore
l'avare ayant ouvert son coffre
avait rassasié son regard
mille ans après
tombe toujours la pluie
sur un village.

## End of a Century

A fly walked on the initial
of a sheet heavy with silence
they woke the child
a thirty-first of December
to see the end of a century
worn-out faces
softened in the glimmer of flames;
gathers, laces, braids
would last for a few months yet
the miser had opened his coffer
and feasted his eyes
a thousand years later
the rain still falls
on a village.

## Autre Temps

Arrière et devant de la maison
ne s'éclairent pas au même instant
l'ombre du feuillage clair
tombe sur un corps
jusqu'à son dernier jour
mais peut-être vient le temps
que le roc seul demeurera
sous la pluie
sans que la moindre chair tressaille
comme dans ce temps des fusillés.

## Another Time

Back and front of the house
are not lit at the same moment
the shadow of pale foliage
falls on a body
until its last day
but a time may be coming
when only the rock will be left
under the rain
and no flesh at all shudder
as now at the shootings.

*Repas*

Dans l'assiette blanche
un peu ébréchée
on mange un morceau de viande saignante
la femme assoiffante
on ne la voit plus.
Sur la route bleue
puis qui devient rouge
de grands chiens passent
comme s'ils avaient
moyen d'exister
durant tous les temps
en portant collier à plaque de cuivre
au nom de leur maître
et sans peur de la nuit.

## Meal

From the white plate
somewhat chipped
a piece of bleeding meat is eaten
the wife who made throats run dry
is no more to be seen.
On the blue road
that turns red a bit later
big dogs pass
as though they had
some way of existing
in all seasons
wearing their master's name
on their brass collars
and with no fear of the night.

## Le Costume du soir

Sur le sol raviné
d'un paysage rafraîchi
un intrépide marcheur
pourvu par la charité
d'un vieux costume du soir
sent venir la mort
pour assez tard encore,
un fil s'est dépris de l'étoffe.
Donateur du vêtement noir
l'architecte va mener son pont
jusqu'à l'achèvement,
museau contre terre à ses pieds
un animal se repose
inconscient d'être né.

## The Evening Suit

Over the eroded earth
of a cooled landscape
an intrepid walker
whom charity has provided
with an old evening suit
feels death on the way
but not for some time yet,
a thread has pulled loose from the cloth.
Donor of the black garment
the architect will bring
his bridge to completion;
muzzle to earth at his feet
an animal rests
unaware of having been born.

*Songerie creuse*

A celui qui pense au néant
on fit pourtant voir
les jeux multiples
des ombres
drapeaux au-dessus d'hommes armés
carrefours au soleil voilé
laines douces aux mains vives
tresses de cheveux ornées
de rubans déchirants
battant de porte ouvert sur les champs
carreau de fenêtre
où frappe le fou serviable
pour héler en passant
un morne habitant.

## Hollow Daydream

He who thinks of nothingness
was shown nevertheless
the multiple tricks
of shadows
flags above armed men
crossroads in veiled sunlight
soft wool in nimble hands
braided hair adorned
with tattered ribbons
door-fold open onto fields
windowpane
at which the obliging simpleton
knocks in passing
to hail a gloomy occupant.

## Spectacle

Dans une fête
fut simplement montré
lent et poussif
le monstre à longs bras.
Sur la place entourée
d'un cirque de collines
il but en renversant sa tête rouge
où collait un bonnet.
Ainsi aimèrent-ils le voir
pour penser de plus près
à de clairs herbages
à leur vie avertie
leur mort elle-même
préservant l'espoir.

*Show*

At a fair
the one-armed monster
slow and short of breath
was simply displayed.
On the square surrounded
by tiers of hills he drank
throwing back his red head
with the cap sticking to it.
They loved to see him that way
it made them feel closer
to green pastures
to their shrewd life,
their death itself
preserving hope.

## La Place

On entend sur la place les cris d'une femme
au soir de l'existence
seule avec sa chevelure
son dédain âpre et pur.
Des pâtres, des vachers
l'ont dans sa jeunesse embrassée.
Demeurent des plafonds noirs
des balcons historiés
faisant le tour de la place
et l'heureux conducteur
d'une voiture vide.

## The Square

On the square one hears the cries of a woman
at the evening of existence
alone with her hair
her sour and pure disdain.
Shepherds, cowherds
kissed her in her youth.
The black ceilings are still there
the balconies with their ornaments
all around the square
and the happy driver
of an empty car.

*Palais souterrain*

Au-dessus d'un palais ancien
enfoui sous la plaine
marche une serve
des insectes armés
sous ses pieds meurent
sauf quelques-uns blessés
qui survivront jusqu'au soleil bas
dans l'heure qu'un homme
avide de civet sombre
emporte à son épaule
la bêche du fossoyeur.
Il faudra encore des ans
avant que le monument
ne soit exhumé
du sol rouge ravagé
par pluies et vents.

## Underground Palace

Above an ancient palace
buried under the plain
a woman is walking
a serf
armed insects
die under her feet
except for a few
wounded
who will live till the sun is low
and the hour when a man
hungry for dark jugged hare
heaves to his shoulder
the grave-digger's spade.
It will still be years
before the monument
is disinterred
from the red soil ravaged
by rains and winds.

## Couple

L'homme sortit pour voir
la peau de sa compagne tressaillit
près des fleurs jamais nue
sauf ce soir
passèrent les herses flamboyantes;
retourné dans la pièce à tout faire
il contempla un visage
un torse usés à peine
la robe déposée
un instant lui sembla
comme le drapeau noir
au temps de l'anarchie
et des vieux parents.

## Couple

The man went out to look
his companion's skin shivered
near flowers never naked
except this evening
the flashing harrows went past;
back in the room used
for everything he studied a face
and torso hardly worn
the dress laid aside
for a moment looked to him
like the black flag
in the days of anarchy
and old parents.

## Signes

Quand un client parfois dans un restaurant sombre
décortique une amande
une main vient se poser sur son étroite épaule
il hésite à finir son verre
la forêt au loin repose sous les neiges
la servante robuste a pâli
il lui faut bien laisser tomber la nuit d'hiver
n'a-t-elle pas souvent vu
à la page dernière
d'un livre à modeste savoir
le mot fin imprimé
en capitales ornées?

*Signs*

Sometimes when a customer in a shadowy restaurant
is shelling an almond
a hand comes to rest on his narrow shoulder
he hesitates to finish his glass
the forest in the distance is resting under its snows
the sturdy waitress has turned pale
he will have to let the winter night fall
has she not often seen
on the last page
of a book of modest learning
the word *end* printed
in ornate capitals?

*Eve*

Un livre déclare Eve
venir de la racine hayah
voulant dire vivre
cependant que des créatures
certaines d'exister
font apprendre aux filles
les passions humaines
mais la plus jeune
tient une pomme blonde
sur un seuil creusé
ne faisant rien d'autre
avant son sommeil.

*Eve*


One book has it that Eve
came from the *haya* root
meaning to live
meanwhile creatures
sure of their existence
pass on to girls knowledge
of human passions
but the youngest
holds a blond apple
on a worn sill
and does nothing else
before she goes to sleep.

*Exil*

Le soir ils écoutent
la même musique à peine gaie
un visage se montre
à un tournant du monde habité
les roses éclosent
une cloche a tinté sous les nuées
devant l'entrée à piliers.
Un homme assis répète à tout venant
dans son velours gris
montrant les sillons à ses mains
moi vivant personne ne touchera
à mes chiens amis.

*Exile*


In the evening they listen to the same
music no one could call merry
a face appears at a corner
of the inhabited world
the roses open
a bell has rung under the clouds
in front of the pillared doorway.
A seated man says to all comers
in his gray velvet
showing his furrowed hands
as long as I live no one
touches my dogs my friends.

## Viande noire

Autour de pierres appelées précieuses
que seulement use
leur propre poussière
les mangeurs de venaison
silencieusement coupent
leur viande noire
les arbres à l'horizon
imitent en leur dessin
une phrase géante.

## Black Meat

Around stones called precious
which only their own
dust can wear down
the eaters of venison
carve in silence
their black meat
the trees on the horizon
imitate in outline
a giant sentence.

## Hameau impérial

Au hameau qu'entourent des seigles
on garde encore un air propice
aux cérémonies
les portes restent ouvertes.
Le mot liberté
inscrit sur la pierre
se reflète dans une glace brisée.
Les racines d'un arbre
sortent d'une terre rongée.
Une des maisons
possède deux lampes
un habitant se couvre
du vêtement à doublure écarlate
de son temps de jeunesse.

## Imperial Hamlet

In the hamlet in the rye fields
they still preserve an air
that invites ceremony
the doors stand open.
The word *liberty*
engraved in a stone
is reflected in a broken mirror.
The roots of a tree
stand out of the scuffed ground.
One of the houses
has two lamps
someone who lives there is putting on
a garment lined with scarlet
from the days of his youth.

## Solitaires

Toujours leur porte s'ouvre mal
derrière eux s'endort la bête
couleur de feu
au seul pas d'homme ou de femme
ils reconnaissent qui passe
sur la route tournante
regardent un instant
pendant du plafond noir
la lampe ornée
une plante verte ocellée meurt
pleure un enfant perdu
sous le vaste ciel bas
puis il neige enfin.

## Solitaries

Their doors always open badly
behind them the fire-colored
animal is asleep
they know whoever passes
on the curving road
man or woman just by the footstep
they watch for a moment
the ornate lamp
hanging from the black ceiling
a spotted green plant is dying
a lost child cries
under the vast low sky
then at last it snows.

## Bout du monde

Au bout du monde
sur une terre éraillée
l'un parle des fleurs décorant
les faïences d'Argonne
au rouge qui les teint on mêle
l'or de vieux ducats hollandais
que l'eau régale attaque.
Comme la nuit vient vite
répond l'autre
par le temps qui court
en ce pays vague.

## World's End

At the world's end
on worn-out ground
the one talks of the flowers
adorning Argonne china
in their red pigment is mixed
the gold of old Dutch ducats
dissolved in aqua regia.
How soon the night falls
the other answers
time goes so fast
in this empty country.

## Tragique du Temps

La porte si forte des prisons
le vent passe dessous quand même
parfois aussi un pâle soleil
en un vieux temps nuance les plis
d'une robe de bourreau.
Dans un bourg de vacances
commence à jouer une harmonie
tandis qu'ayant posé sa houe
assis un journalier contemple
les exécutants pacifiques
voués au massacre
dans l'année
disant croire à leurs âmes éternelles
à leur corps ressuscitant.

## The Tragic in Time

So strong the prison doors
but the wind gets under
and at moments a pale sun
in an old time picks out the folds
of an executioner's robe.
In a resort town
they strike up a tune
meanwhile having set down his hoe
a seated day-laborer watches
the peaceful executants
all to be massacred
within the year
who claim to believe in their immortal souls
and the resurrection of the body.

## Larron

Le coeur des vaches bat dans le pré
un homme y vient voler leur lait
marchant dans la fraîcheur de la rosée
il n'aime ni ne hait
pour lui seul s'arrête le temps
le soleil arrivé haut dans le ciel
alors il ne peut que dormir
répudiant
enfance, âge adulte, vieillesse.
S'il passe rien ne sert de crier:
Attendez.

## Thief

The cows' hearts beat in the meadow
a man comes to steal their milk
walking in the cool of the dew
he neither loves nor hates
time stops just for him
when the sun is high in the sky
all he can do then is sleep
sloughing off
childhood, maturity, old age.
If he passes it's no use calling:
Wait.

## About the Author

Jean Follain was born at Canisy, in Normandy, in 1903. He studied law at the Faculté de Caen and graduated with honors. As a student he was also interested in history, particularly that of the nineteenth century. In 1925 he went to Paris to continue his studies. There his life and literary beginnings were both quiet. He associated with a group that included Max Jacob, Pierre Reverdy, and Léon-Paul Fargue, and his poems were published in several literary reviews. His first substantial book of poems, *La Main chaude*, was published in 1933. Among his subsequent books of poems (as represented in this selection) are *Chants terrestres* (1937), *Ici-bas* (1941), *Transparence du monde* (1943), *Exister* (1947), *Territoires* (1953), *Des heures* (1960), *Appareil de la terre* (1964), and *D'après tout* (1967). Follain died in 1971.

## About the Translator

W.S. Merwin was born in New York City in 1927 and grew up in New Jersey and Pennsylvania. From 1949 to 1951 he worked as a tutor in France, Majorca, and Portugal and has since lived in many parts of the world, translating and writing poetry. His many awards include the Pulitzer Prize in Poetry, the Tanning Prize for Mastery in the Art of Poetry, the Bollingen Prize, the Ruth Lilly Poetry Prize, the Lenore Marshall Prize for poetry, the Lila Wallace–Reader's Digest Writers' Award, and the Governor's Award for Literature in the State of Hawaii, as well as fellowships from the Academy of American Poets (for which he was formerly a chancellor), the Guggenheim Foundation, the National Endowment for the Arts, and the Rockefeller Foundation. He is the author of many books of poetry and translation. He and his wife live in Hawaii, where he cultivates rare and endangered palm trees.

The Chinese character for poetry is made up of two parts: "word" and "temple." It also serves as pressmark for Copper Canyon Press.

Founded in 1972, Copper Canyon Press remains dedicated to publishing poetry exclusively, from Nobel laureates to new and emerging authors. The Press thrives with the generous patronage of readers, writers, booksellers, librarians, teachers, students, and funders — everyone who shares the conviction that poetry invigorates the language and sharpens our appreciation of the world.

PUBLISHERS' CIRCLE

The Allen Foundation for the Arts
Lannan Foundation
National Endowment for the Arts

EDITORS' CIRCLE

The Breneman Jaech Foundation
Cynthia Hartwig and Tom Booster
Emily Warn and Daj Oberg
Washington State Arts Commission

*For information and catalogs:*

COPPER CANYON PRESS
Post Office Box 271
Port Townsend, Washington 98368
360/385-4925
www.coppercanyonpress.org

This book is set in Stempel Garamond (1924) based on type specimens from 1592 with roman type cut by Claude Garamond and italic type cut by Robert Granjon. Book design by Valerie Brewster, Scribe Typography. Printed at Bookmobile.